Helping Children See Jesus

ISBN: 978-1-64104-009-9

God Is Omniscient
Trusting in the All-Knowing God
Old Testament Volume 28: Esther

Authors: Lois S. Sulahian, Janet Master
Illustrator: Vernon Henkel
Computer Graphic Artist: Sean Tweed
Page Layout: Morgan Melton, Patricia Pope

© 2018 Bible Visuals International
PO Box 153, Akron, PA 17501-0153
Phone: (717) 859-1131
www.biblevisuals.org

All rights reserved. No part of this publication may be reproduced, stored in a retrieval system or transmitted in any form by any means, electronic, mechanical, photocopy, recording or otherwise, without the prior permission of the publisher, except as provided by USA copyright law.

RELATED ITEMS

To access related items (such as activities, memory verse posters and translated texts) please visit our web store at www.biblevisuals.org and enter 2028 at the top right of the web page. You may need to reduce the zoom setting to get the search box.

FREE TEXT DOWNLOAD

To obtain a FREE printable copy of the English teaching text (PDF format) under Product Format, please scroll down and select Extra–PDF Teacher Text Download. Then under Language select English before clicking the ADD TO CART button to place in your shopping cart. Other languages are available at an additional cost from the Language menu. When checking out, use coupon code XTACSV17 at checkout and click on Apply Coupon to receive the discount on the English text.

Lesson 1
GOD KNOWS THE NEED

NOTE TO THE TEACHER

The Old Testament books are divided into four groups:

> Books of the Law (Genesis through Deuteronomy)
> Books of History (Joshua through Esther)
> Books of Poetry (Job through Song of Solomon)
> Books of the Prophets (Isaiah through Malachi)

These 39 books were not all written in the indexed order. Certain books were written at approximately the same time, as follows:

Genesis, Job	2 Kings, 2 Chronicles, Obadiah, Joel, Jonah, Amos, Hosea, Micah, Isaiah, Nahum, Zephaniah, Habakkuk, Jeremiah, Lamentations
Exodus, Leviticus	
Numbers, Deuteronomy	
Joshua	
Judges, Ruth	
1 Samuel	
2 Samuel, Psalms	Daniel, Ezekiel
1 Kings, 1 Chronicles, Song of Solomon, Proverbs, Ecclesiastes	Ezra, Esther, Haggai, Zechariah
	Nehemiah, Malachi

Keep a copy of this list in your notebook. Refer to it frequently. Observe that the books of Ezra and Esther were writtenat the same time. Esther's experiences fit exactly between chapters 6 and 7 of Ezra. (See Old Testament Volume 27.)

The Jews had been captives of the Babylonians and the Persians. A new Persian king gave the Israelites their freedom. Only about 50,000 of them elected to return to Jerusalem. Many, including Esther and her relatives, chose to stay in Persia. God knows everything. He knew that in time those who remainedcould be destroyed. To preserve them, He would use Esther, a Jewish girl.

The name of God is not mentioned in the book of Esther. Yet He is in the book. His sovereignty and loving care for His people are obvious. Carefully observe the precise timing of events. As you teach these lessons, continually emphasize the omniscience of God. On a poster print in large letters: *God Is Omniscient.* Add definition: *God Knows Everything.*

As you introduce and review the memory verse, display the poster. Hold it aloft whenever a lesson event emphasizes this truth.

The Lord God created the universe: heavens, earth, everything, everyone. He has perfect knowledge of all His creation (Job 37:16). He knows all that will occur and when it will occur (Acts 15:18). He is omniscient. He knew all about Esther. He knows all about you, Teacher, and each of your students. Make this glorious truth live!

Scripture to be studied: Esther 1:1—2:20; Psalm 139:1-4, 13-16

The *aim* of the lesson: God knows all about everything.

> **What your students should *know*:** God has given each of us certain abilities. We should use these gifts to serve Him.
>
> **What your students should *feel*:** Thankful that God loved us enough to plan for us.
>
> **What your students should *do*:** Determine right now to serve God throughout their lives.

Lesson outline (for the teacher's and students' notebooks):

1. The king's ambitious plan (Esther 1:1-9).
2. The king's proud demand (Esther 1:10-22).
3. The king's search (Esther 2:1-14).
4. The king's new queen (Esther 2:15-20).

The verse to be memorized:

> God . . . knows all things. (1 John 3:20)

THE LESSON

Do you know anyone who is especially beautiful? Pretty girls often receive much attention. Contests are sometimes held to decide which girl is loveliest. Today's lesson describes a beauty contest held hundreds of years ago. The winner won something many girls wanted. And she became important in history. Listen carefully!

Many of God's people, the Israelites, were living in Persia. Years before, the Lord had punished them for disobedience. Their land had been conquered. And the people were taken as captives to a foreign land. There they settled to rear their families. Years later, some wanted to return to their homeland. And the king gave them permission to go. Many, however, were content to live in Persia. Life was easy for them now. They were no longer slaves. Indeed, many owned land and held important government positions.

1. THE KING'S AMBITIOUS PLAN
Esther 1:1-9

Ahasuerus was the king of Persia. His empire stretched from India to Ethiopia. (Show back cover map.) He ruled 127 provinces. But that was not enough for Ahasuerus. He wanted to conquer the land of Greece. So he invited to the palace his princes and army officers. He thought, I shall show them how rich and strong our kingdom is. Then they will gladly fight for me.

Ahasuerus planned a great feast for his leaders. The celebration would last six months. Six months–imagine that!

Show Illustration #1

The palace was magnificent. Colorful flags flew. Servants hurried here and there. Some carried trays of dates, raisins, and honey cakes. Others brought earthen pots full of wine. Guests sat on benches of gold and silver. Each drank from a special golden cup.

The sounds of music and happy feasting were everywhere. What a tremendous party! Now the leaders would fight for King Ahasuerus. And they would surely win the war. Greece would soon belong to Persia.

The great part of this celebration came the final week. The ordinary men of the city were then invited to the palace. After all, they too were going to be sent to war. Nobles, generals, and commoners would fight against the Greeks. So together they enjoyed the festivities.

Meanwhile, Queen Vashti entertained the ladies of Susa in her part of the palace.

2. THE KING'S PROUD DEMAND
Esther 1:10-22

The week of feasting reached its climax. The king was drunk. So were most of his men, doubtless. The king sent the queen an order. "Come show your beauty to all the men!" he commanded. This sounds innocent–almost like a compliment. But Persian customs were different from others. No high-born woman paraded before nobles. Dancing girls or slaves did that. But certainly not a royal queen! To make matters worse, ordinary men of town were present. So actually the drunken king had insulted Queen Vashti.

Show Illustration #2

The queen sent a reply through a messenger. "Tell the king I refuse to come!" she said.

The servant trembled. Terrified, he trudged to the banquet hall. No one ever refused the king!

When King Ahasuerus heard Vashti's refusal, he was furious. "Does the queen dare to disobey me?" he screamed. He, the king of Persia, had been humiliated–by a woman!

The king called together his wise men, the lawmakers. They were worried about the king's problem. "Vashti must be punished!" they decided. "If she is not, our wives will follow her example. Soon every wife in the land will disobey her husband. This cannot be!"

So they discussed a plan. The leader spoke for all: "We shall write a new law for the king. Vashti will be sent away forever. Then the king can find a better queen. All wives everywhere must obey their husbands."

Ahasuerus liked their idea. So the law was written, and runners took the decree to every part of the kingdom. Once a Persian law was written, it could never be changed. From now on, all wives would have to obey their husbands!

3. THE KING'S SEARCH
Esther 2:1-14

Ahasuerus had to get busy with plans for conquering Greece. It was a long process–the preparation, the journey, the wearisome battle. But the invasion failed. The Persians were defeated. And King Ahasuerus returned home dejected.

Ahasuerus moped about the palace. He had no one to comfort him. He thought, *How beautiful Vashti was! But I shall never again see her. I have many wives, but no one special to be queen.*

The king's men had a suggestion. "Let beautiful young women be sought for the king. We shall have a contest to find the most beautiful girl. She can be the new queen."

The king was delighted. Servants were sent throughout the vast empire. They searched diligently. They brought many lovely girls to the palace. Some came happily, each hoping to become queen. Others had to be snatched from their parents' homes. They did not want to join the king's crowd of wives. But all had to come. For a whole year the young women prepared for the pageant.

Show Illustration #3

Among the girls picked for the contest was Esther. She was from the capital city, Susa. She was different from the others in several ways. First, she was an Israelite, a Jewess. Being Jewish, she worshiped the true and living God of Heaven. She had nothing to do with the Persians' false gods.

Esther was also an orphan. Her parents had died when she was young. So she was adopted and reared by a cousin named Mordecai. Mordecai loved Esther as his own daughter. God had given Esther this cousin to teach her about Himself. Before she left for the palace, Mordecai gave Esther a warning. "Do not tell anyone who your relatives are. Never mention that you are Jewish!" (See Esther 2:20.)

The Lord also made Esther beautiful. He who knows about His whole creation, knew about Esther. Before she was born, He knew what she would be like. And God knows about you (Psalm 139:15-16)! God made Esther beautiful for a particular purpose. Her beauty was part of His plan.

4. THE KING'S NEW QUEEN
Esther 2:15-20

Esther is a Persian name which means "star." She now became the star of a thrilling story.

Esther had begun her year of training at the palace. She was sweet and kind. So the servant in charge liked her. He gave her the best rooms and seven maids. Even so, Esther did not feel above the others. She knew she had done nothing to deserve her beauty.

Finally the time came for Esther to meet the king. For months she had been preparing for this day. She was allowed to choose whatever clothing and jewelry she desired. Esther could have grasped the best gown and the most gorgeous jewels. Instead, she turned to the wise old keeper of the women. "Will you please decide for me?" she asked. Together they chose her outfit.

At last Esther was ready. She smiled at the servants and the other contestants. Everyone gasped with delight. Esther [Star] glowed like a million stars! Her heart pounded as she approached the throne room. *Will the king approve me?* she wondered.

Ahasuerus was waiting on his throne. He had seen many pretty girls. Still he was lonely. The door opened and there stood Esther. Immediately the king loved her. He knew he had found his queen.

"Bring a crown!" he commanded. "Prepare a feast!"

Show Illustration #4

"I choose Esther," he announced. "Esther is the beautiful new queen of Persia." Standing, King Ahasuerus placed a crown on Esther's head.

God gave obedient, humble Esther the honored place in the kingdom. She did not tell anyone–not even the king– that she was Jewish. She, the queen, remembered Mordecai's command and obeyed him.

Because of Esther's being queen, Mordecai stayed near the palace. Usually he sat at the king's gate. There he heard and saw all that happened around the palace. He, a Jew, was a trusted workman of Persian royalty.

The Lord God knows everything. He knew all about Esther. He had created her beautiful. He knew she would be an orphan. And He had a special plan for her.

Did you know that God created you carefully and lovingly? He did; He really, truly did. He knew all about you before you were born. And He knows all about you now. He even knows the number of hairs on your head (Matthew 10:30)! He has given you particular abilities. He understands you. He knows exactly what you can be and do for Him. God, the omniscient One, knows *everything!*

What talents has God given you? Do you have artistic ability? Can you sing well or play an instrument? What skill do you have? Could God now use this—His gift to you? If so how? In what way could God use your talent later in life?

Remember: Esther was always humble. She remembered her abilities and beauty were from the Lord. She never boasted, "I am the most beautiful. The king chose me."

Esther also kept obeying her foster-father, Mordecai. She never argued saying, "I am the queen. I can do as I please." Are you obedient as Esther was? The Word of God is filled with truths we should learn. By reading the Bible daily, we learn to obey God. And we learn to obey those whom God appoints over us. (For example: parents, teacher, employer.) God, who knows all, chooses humble, obedient servants.

Lesson 2
GOD KNOWS THE PROBLEMS

NOTE TO THE TEACHER

God knows everything. He knows all that is happening throughout the universe right now. He knows everything that will take place in the future.

The eternal God "appointeth the number of the stars; He calleth them all by their names. Great is our Lord, and of great power; His understanding is infinite" (Psalm 147:4-5). "The eyes of the Lord are in every place, beholding the evil and the good" (Proverbs 15:3). It is an encouragement and comfort to know that God is omniscient. The Lord Jesus said, "Are not two sparrows sold for less than a penny? And one of them shall not fall on the ground without your Father. But the very hairs of your head are all numbered. Fear not, therefore; you are of more value than many sparrows." God is the One who knows all.

Did the events of the book of Esther surprise God? NO! He knew that King Ahasuerus would promote the wicked Haman. The Lord knew that Haman was an enemy of the Jews (Esther 3:10). God knew why Haman hated the Jews. Haman was an Agagite (3:10). Once there was a man named Agag. He was king of the savage Amalekites (1 Samuel 15:8, 33). Nine hundred years before the time of Esther, the Amalekites attacked the Jews. Cruelly they killed old people, women, and children. (See Exodus 17:8-16; Deuteronomy 25:17-19.) God commanded King Saul (500 years after the time of Agag) to destroy all the Amalekites. Even the Amalekites' animals were to be slain. But Saul (first king of the Jews) did not obey God perfectly. (Study 1 Samuel 15:1-35.) Thus the Amalekites lived on. And their descendants always hated the Jews.

Mordecai, cousin of Esther, was a Jew. He was descended from Kish (Esther 2:5). Kish's son, Saul, became the Jews' first king (1 Samuel 10:1-2). Why did Mordecai refuse to bow before Haman? Perhaps because his ancestors and Haman's ancestors hated each other. (See Exodus 17:14-16; Deuteronomy 25:19.) Or maybe Haman claimed to have divine powers. Mordecai, a faithful Jew, could not–would not–honor mere man. (See Deuteronomy 6:13-14.)

When Haman learned that Mordecai was a Jew, he was furious. He determined to destroy Mordecai–and every Jew. Could he exterminate these people of God? No, he could not! Others since Haman have also tried to dispose of all Jews. They have murdered millions of Jewish people. But God chose the Jews for Himself because He loves them (Deuteronomy 7:7-8). So He always has His eye on them everywhere (Psalm 139:7-8). The Lord also knows you, Teacher. He knows every one of your students. He knows all about them. Remember–God is omniscient!

Scripture to be studied: Esther 2:21-5:8; Psalm 139:5-12

The *aim* of the lesson: To help students understand that God has placed them where they are.

What your students should *know*: God knows everything that happens to us. We can therefore trust Him even in difficult or dangerous places.

What your students should *feel*: A desire to obey God despite opposition.

What your students should *do*: Ask God to help them to be faithful to Him in difficulties.

Lesson outline (for the teacher's and students' notebooks):
1. Mordecai's challenge (Esther 2:21-3:4).
2. Haman's conspiracy (Esther 3:5-15).
3. Mordecai's grief (Esther 4:1-14).
4. Esther's obedience (Esther 4:15-5:8).

The verse to be memorized:
God . . . knows all things. (1 John 3:20)

THE LESSON

God knows everything. God knew that Esther was a Jew. But King Ahasuerus did not know that. Nor did Esther tell him. Although she was queen, she continued to obey her cousin Mordecai. (See Esther 2:20.) One day Mordecai learned something dreadful.

1. MORDECAI'S CHALLENGE
Esther 2:21-3:4

Two palace guards were whispering. They were wildly angry at King Ahasuerus. Why? We do not know. But there was One who knew. Who was that? *(The living God of Heaven. He knows everything.)* Mordecai, sitting at the king's gate, heard the guards' evil decision. "We shall kill the king!" they snarled.

Mordecai immediately rushed the awful news to Queen Esther. Esther relayed the word to King Ahasuerus. The king sent detectives to investigate the plot. The report was found to be true. And the two guilty men were hanged on a gallows.

All this was recorded in the king's diary. But for some strange reason, nothing was done to reward Mordecai.

Mordecai was pleased that Esther was queen. Yet he missed her brightness in his home. He seldom saw her now. She lived in a separate part of the palace. Only the king's wives and their servants could enter there.

The day came when King Ahasuerus did promote a man. No, not Mordecai. The king appointed Haman to be his assistant. Haman thus became the second most powerful man in the kingdom. The king gave a command: "All the king's servants, attention! You are to kneel before Haman and give him high honor."

Mordecai was shocked! Persian kings, he knew, claimed to be god-like. Apparently Haman was also thought to have god-like powers. Mordecai was a faithful Jew. Jews gave high honor to God alone (Deuteronomy 6:13-14). Whenever Haman passed by, all the king's servants bowed down.

Show Illustration #5

That is, all knelt except Mordecai. He stood erect. This made Haman furious.

Day after day the king's men honored Haman. Mordecai did not. Each time they questioned him. "Mordecai, why do you disobey the command of the king?"

Mordecai finally whispered, "I am a Jew. We Jews give such honor only to the living God of Heaven."

The officials ran to Haman. "Mordecai does not bow before you because he is a Jew."

"A *Jew!*" Haman hissed. "I must get rid of him. For a moment he thought. Then the enraged Haman shouted, "Mordecai and ALL Jews must die."

2. HAMAN'S CONSPIRACY
Esther 3:5-15

Haman finally decided how the Jews should die. But he did not know when. So the lot [Pur] was cast, like today, when some people throw dice. Haman had to know the exact month for destroying all Jews. The lot showed that the month Adar (February/March on our calendar) was the time. That gave wicked Haman almost a year to complete his plans.

How can I get this approved by the king? Haman wondered. His enormous hate made him clever.

Show Illustration #6

When he was able to see Ahasuerus, he spoke smoothly. "O king, live forever! Some people scattered throughout your kingdom have laws different from yours. In fact, they have their own set of laws. They could be dangerous. Your majesty would be wise to do away with these people. A law should be made that they be destroyed." Then Haman whispered, "I shall pay the cost of killing them."

A bit of what Haman said was right. The Jews did follow the laws of God. But only *one* Jew, Mordecai, had broken only one Persian law. He refused to kneel before Haman. Yet Haman convinced the king that all Jews were lawbreakers. Actually, the Jews had lived peaceably in Persia for many years.

King Ahasuerus replied, "Plan the execution any way you wish. Here is my ring to seal the law." He had not even asked who had disobeyed his laws! With the king's ring, Haman could sign anything in the king's name. Soon the king's messengers raced through the city. To every province they carried copies of the new law. This law was written in the name of King Ahasuerus. It was sealed with his ring. But actually the law was Haman's!

Haman's law was read everywhere. "Destroy, kill, and annihilate all the Jews! All are to be slain–young and old, women and little children. Execute them on the thirteenth day of the month Adar. Seize all their belongings for yourselves."

Now, what would the Jews–God's people–do? Did the Lord know all that was happening? Had he known of Haman's evil law? *(Yes!)* The Lord God sees *your* dangers and problems, too. He knows *all*–and He is always in control.

3. MORDECAI'S GRIEF
Esther 4:1-14

Mordecai tore his clothes. With ashes on his head, he went to the king's gate. There he wailed loudly as if people had already died. Throughout the entire kingdom, every Jew wept bitterly. But they could do nothing to protect themselves. A law sealed with the king's ring could not be changed.

Esther learned that Mordecai was at the palace gate in rags. She sent him new clothes. But he refused to accept them. Esther did not understand Mordecai's great sadness, for she had not heard of Haman's law.

Show Illustration #7

Mordecai sent Esther a copy of the awful law. He added a personal message. "Haman will have every Jew destroyed. Esther, you are the queen. You must go to the king. Plead with him to save our people."

Esther answered, "I cannot do that! No one can go to the king without being invited. He is guarded in the throne room. Anyone who enters without permission is killed immediately. A visitor is safe only if the king holds out the golden scepter. The king has not called for me in a month. I am sorry. I cannot go."

Mordecai responded to Esther at once. "Do you suppose you are safe in the palace? Remember! Every Jew in the whole kingdom is to be slain. You will be found out to be Jewish. They will kill you, too. You must try to save our people. Speak to the king. The Jews must be saved. Somebody has to come to our rescue. They could be delivered by another. But you and your relatives will die. Who knows? Maybe you have been chosen queen for this very important purpose."

Mordecai remembered that the Lord knows everything. He understood that the Jews were chosen by God for Himself. Mordecai was assured the all-knowing One would save His people. But how?

If you had been Esther, what would you have done? Encourage discussion.)

4. ESTHER'S OBEDIENCE
Esther 4:15-5:8

Esther sent her answer to Mordecai. "Gather together all the Jews in the city of Susa. Fast for me. Do not eat or drink for three days and nights. My maids and I will also fast. Then, against the law, I shall go to the king. And if I perish, I perish."

In those days, fasting included praying. (See Ezra 8:23.)

Show Illustration #8

For three days and nights Esther and her maids prayed. So did Mordecai and the Jews in the city. Oh, how they prayed! And prayed. And prayed. They were really serious about this matter.

On the third day, Esther was dressed in her best. She wore her royal robes of authority and power. With racing heart, she walked slowly, quietly, to the king's hall. When Ahasuerus saw his queen, he was delighted. Smiling, he held out the golden scepter to her. (Show front cover illustration.) Esther was safe!

"What is it, Queen Esther?" the king asked. "What would you like to have? I will give you as much as half of my kingdom!"

Esther replied, "I have prepared a banquet for you, O king. Will you please come today–and bring Haman with you?"

Why would Esther risk her life to ask this? the king wondered. *What does Haman have to do with her urgent request?*

The king spoke to his personal servant. "Bring Haman quickly so we may do what Esther asks."

Do you think the king was curious? Are *you?*

For a moment, suppose you had been Mordecai. You were responsible for saving the king's life. Because of your report, two guards were hung. How would you have felt about that? (Have discussion.)

Would you have been disappointed not to have received a reward? Why?

What would you have done when Haman was promoted? Why?

How would you have reacted to Haman's death sentence upon you and all Jews?

Now try to imagine that you are Esther. You are young. You have just been made responsible (by Mordecai) for saving every Jew in all the kingdom. How would you feel about this?

At such an urgent time, would you have argued with Mordecai? Why?

Would it have bothered you to have to go to the king? Why? If the name of God was never mentioned, would you have thought of Him? Why?

Ours is a tremendous universe. Our world is huge with more people than can be pictured. There are also planets and stars, galaxies, moon and sun. With all there is everywhere, God knows about you. How do you feel about this? Why?

Teacher: Enter here your own responses to the foregoing questions.

Lesson 3
GOD KNOWS THE GOOD AND THE EVIL

NOTE TO THE TEACHER

King David lived about 400 years before Queen Esther. One of his Psalms (139) contains truths found in the book of Esther. What David says of himself, you can say of yourself:

God knows me (Psalm 139:1).
He knows when I sit down and stand up (v. 2).
He understands my thoughts (v. 2).
He knows all my ways (v. 3).
He knows beforehand the words I shall speak (v. 4).
His knowledge is too wonderful for me (v. 6).

God knows everything. "The Lord knows the way of the righteous" (Psalm 1:6). "The Lord is good, a stronghold in the day of trouble; and He knows those who trust in Him" (Nahum 1:7). ". . . The Lord knows those who are His" (2 Timothy 2:19).

God knows His own family. Whatever happens to His children is no surprise to Him. He knows all the past, the present, and the future. These are glorious truths for the children of God.

But what about those who have not trusted in Christ Jesus? Does the Lord God know about them? Indeed, He does! "The eyes of the Lord are in every place, beholding the evil and the good" (Proverbs 15:3). That which comforts and challenges believers should terrify unbelievers. "It is a fearful thing to fall into the hands of the living God" (Hebrews 10:31).

God knows all about you, Teacher. He knows your students. Whether they are good (like Mordecai) or evil (like Haman), God knows. Help each one to grasp this tremendous truth: God is omniscient.

Scripture to be studied: Esther 5:9-7:10; Psalm 139:17-19

The *aim* of the lesson: To teach that God knows the future.

What your students should *know*: God knows when things will happen.

What your students should *feel*: Perfect joy in belonging to the all-knowing One.

What your students should *do*:
Saved: Pray to do what God wills.
Unsaved: Receive the Lord Jesus and pray to walk in God's ways.

Lesson outline (for the teacher's and students' notebooks):
1. A foolish boast (Esther 5:9-14).
2. A sleepless king (Esther 6:1-9).
3. An important change (Esther 6:10-14).
4. A quick execution (Esther 7:1-10).

The verse to be memorized:

God . . . knows all things. (1 John 3:20)

THE LESSON
1. A FOOLISH BOAST
Esther 5:9-14

King Ahasuerus was puzzled. His queen had just invited him and Haman to a banquet. *Why has she included Haman? the king wondered. A banquet is held to honor someone. Haman is second in power. Surely Esther would not hold a banquet in his honor. But why did she invite him? Why?*

Turning to a servant, the king commanded, "Bring Haman quickly."

The two, dressed in their best, went to Queen Esther's banquet.

– 23 –

The king and Haman had a marvelous time. The feast was magnificent. The decorations were beautiful. Finally the king asked, "Esther, what would you like to have? I shall give you even half of my kingdom." (Persian kings could give no more than that.)

Queen Esther answered. She spoke slowly and simply. "I trust I have found favor with you, O king. Thank you for coming. Thank you for being willing to do what I ask." Esther hesitated. After a long pause, she spoke again, though less courageously. "Will you, O king, and Haman come tomorrow for another banquet? Then I shall tell you my request."

The king left–more curious than ever. Haman was the happiest he'd ever been. He, Haman, attended Queen Esther's banquet. He and the king were her only guests. And she had invited him to yet another banquet. How pleased–and proud– was Haman!

Mordecai sat outside the palace gate. When Haman passed him, Mordecai did not stand. Nor did he bow down before Haman. Haman, though filled with rage, somehow controlled his temper. At home he called together his friends and his wife.

Show Illustration #9

"I have something to tell only you," he began softly. "I want you to know that I am very rich. You know I have sons. But do you realize I have a total of 10 sons? (See Esther 9:7-10.) Ten sons! Think of it!" Haman's voice became louder. "I cannot tell you how important I am to King Ahasuerus. But I can tell you this: I have been promoted. I am now over all the servants and princes. So I am next to the king in power. And that is not all! Today I attended Queen Esther's banquet. She gave it for only the king and me. And she has invited me–along with the king–for another banquet tomorrow."

"I have all this power," Haman said proudly. Then he frowned. "But what good does it do me? That Jew Mordecai just sits at the palace gate. He does not tremble when he sees me. And he refuses to bow before me. He is insulting me in public."

Haman's wife had an idea with which all his friends agreed. "Since you are now so important, build a huge gallows. Make it 75 feet high–higher than the city walls. Tomorrow, ask the king's permission to hang Mordecai on the gallows. Then he will be dead for all to see. And you can go happily to the queen's banquet."

Haman was delighted. "I shall do it!" he exclaimed. And immediately he gave orders for the gallows to be built.

Haman had everything. He was powerful, rich, and popular. But Haman had more–he was filled with pride. "I, I, I," he said boasting of himself. God heard Haman's bragging. He knew Haman's evil plan. The Lord also knew His people, the Jews. He had His eye on them. But Haman did not know this. So he had spoken proudly and foolishly.

2. A SLEEPLESS KING
Esther 6:1-9

That night King Ahasuerus could not sleep. He tossed and turned. He asked himself one question after another. *Why did Esther risk her life to invite me to her banquet? Why did she want Haman to come? Twice I have offered her half of my kingdom. What more does she want? Why is she having another banquet? Will the second feast be as good as the first?* The king's thoughts kept him wide awake.

Finally he decided there was only one way to fall asleep. He would have the records of the kingdom read to him. The history of Persian affairs would certainly put him to sleep!

Show Illustration #10

The courtier chose one particular book and began to read. He read on and on and on. It was almost morning when the king ordered, "Stop! Read that last part again." The servant read: "Two palace guards schemed to kill King Ahasuerus. Mordecai, the gatekeeper, reported them. The detectives investigated. Mordecai's report was found to be true. The two guilty men were hung on a gallows."

"Is that the end?" the king demanded. "Was nothing done to reward this Mordecai person?"

"No, O king. He was not rewarded or honored in any way."

"I must take care of that at once," the king decided.

At that moment he heard a noise in the courtyard. "Who is in the outer court?" the king demanded.

A servant investigated. "It is Haman," he said.

"Let him come in," the king snapped. Ahasuerus had only one concern right now: *How should I honor Mordecai?*

Haman had had a busy night overseeing the building of the gallows. Now the work was done. Haman wanted to get immediate permission to hang Mordecai. He thought, *I can't wait for the king to get to his throne. Besides, I'm above such formality now. I am the king's special friend. Esther invited only me and the king to her banquets. She realizes how important I am.*

"Haman!" the servant called. "King Ahasuerus says you may come in."

Haman entered, ready to say, "O king, may I have permission..."

But the king spoke first. "Haman, there is someone I want to honor. What should be done for him?"

Haman thought for a moment. *Who would the king want to honor? Why, no one but me, of course! First the queen honors me at her banquets. Now the king will honor me! What would I like him to do for me?*

Haman spoke confidently. "O king, this is how you should honor him. Have your servants bring a royal robe which you have worn. Order also your own horse. Let the robe and horse be entrusted to a royal prince. The prince should put the robe on the man you are honoring. He should lead the man on horseback through the city streets. Have him shout, 'This is the man the king is delighted to honor!'"

3. AN IMPORTANT CHANGE
Esther 6:10-14

"Excellent, Haman! Now go at once," the king commanded. "Get my robe and my horse. Do exactly what you have said for Mordecai the Jew. You know who I mean–he sits at the palace gate. Remember everything you have said and do it for him!"

Haman was shocked. He trudged off, got the robe and put it on Mordecai.

Show Illustration #11

With Mordecai on horseback, Haman made his announcement again and again.

He led Mordecai from one city street to another. Everywhere the crowd heard the same proclamation. "This is done for the man the king is delighted to honor!"

Mordecai's face showed his happiness. Haman's frowns and sagging shoulders showed his humiliation. Did the Lord God know about all this? (Yes!) It is written in His Word: "A man's pride shall bring him low. But honor shall uphold the humble in spirit" (Proverbs 29:23).

Afterward, Mordecai returned to the king's gate. But Haman covered his head and ran home. He told his wife and friends all that had happened.

One of his wise men said, "Mordecai is a Jew. So you are in serious trouble, Haman."

Why do you think he said that? (Allow discussion.) *Haman wanted to kill Mordecai. Now Mordecai was an honored friend of the king. Haman had planned to dispose of all Jews. But the Jews are God's special people.* (See Visualized Bible, Old Testament, Volume 6, Lesson #1.) Would God allow all His people to be slain? Did God know all that was happening? Did He care?

Haman had little time to worry. The king's messengers had come. They led him to Queen Esther's second banquet.

4. A QUICK EXECUTION
Esther 7:1-10

The king and Haman ate another elegant feast with the queen. Finally Ahasuerus said, "Ask what you wish, Queen Esther. You can have it–as much as half of my kingdom."

"O king," the queen began, "have I truly found favor with you? If so, will you please spare my life? And will you spare the life of all my people?" she begged. "I and my people have been sold to be destroyed. We shall be killed–all of us."

King Ahasuerus was stunned. "Who has threatened the life of my queen and her people?"

Show Illustration #12

"Our foe, the enemy, is this vile Haman!" Esther shouted.

There! The kingdom's best-kept secret was out. Queen Esther was a Jew! And Haman had ordered that all Jews were to be slain!

Haman was terrified.

The king was furious. He rushed outside to the palace garden. Pacing back and forth he cried, "My queen, my beautiful queen! What can I do? The Persian laws cannot be changed. There is no way to change them! O Esther! Dear, dear Esther!"

Meanwhile Haman had thrown himself on Esther, pleading, "Save me! Queen Esther, please, please save me!"

Just then the king rushed inside and saw Haman clawing the queen. "Are you molesting my queen right here in my house?" he demanded.

Quickly a servant threw a cover over Haman's face.

Another servant, pointing outside to the gallows, suggested: "Hang him!"

King Ahasuerus shouted: "Hang him on the gallows!"

So Haman was led to the gallows. There he died where he had expected Mordecai to die. Only then did the king calm down.

God, the omniscient One, is sovereign. He is always in control of everything. He knew Haman was proud and evil–and would have destroyed all Jews. He knew Mordecai was humble and wise. He knew Esther would be willing to give her life for the Jews.

God knows all about *you*. If you are His child, He will guide you. He led Esther and Mordecai to do right at the right time. So He will lead you. Will you be willing to let Him do so?

Lesson 4
GOD CAUSES HIS PEOPLE TO TRIUMPH

NOTE TO THE TEACHER

God is nowhere mentioned in the book of Esther. Yet the book shows very clearly that He is the all-knowing One. And He cares for His own. As a result of the king's drunkenness, Queen Vashti had been dismissed. She was replaced on the throne by a Jewish girl, Esther. God knew that wicked Haman would plan to kill all Jews. The Lord knew that Esther would protect the Jews from annihilation. He knew she would courageously risk her life to do so. God knew Ahasuerus would have a sleepless night. God caused the king's servant to read from a particular record book. Having heard that account, the king honored Mordecai. And all the Jews in Persia were preserved. Why? Because the king had not been able to sleep.

God allowed proud Haman to go just so far–no farther. "Pride goeth before destruction, and an haughty spirit before a fall" (Proverbs 16:18). The Lord knew Haman's dice would determine a certain date. That date would later give the Jews time to protect themselves. God knew that, too.

The Lord God knew everything in the long ago. He knows everything today. And He knows all the future. There is never any reason for a child of God to panic. God is sovereign–He controls everything. He is omniscient–He knows everything. He loves you with an everlasting love. (See Jeremiah 31:3.) He can give you His peace through every trial, every persecution. (See Isaiah 26:3-4.) For the Christian life often includes suffering. (See Acts 14:19; 2 Corinthians 11:24-27; 12:7-10; 1 Peter 2:18-23; 4:12-13; 5:8-9.) The Christian life may even include martyrdom (Acts 7:54-60). But remember: God knows everything. He knew, from the very beginning, all that would ever happen. And He loves and is always with His own. (See Psalm 139:7-10; Hebrews 13:5.)

Emphasize these truths!

Scripture to be studied: Esther 8:1—10:3; Psalm 46:1-11; 139:17-24

The *aim* of the lesson: To show your students that God knows and controls nations–and individuals.

What your students should *know*: God knows how to care for His people.

What your students should *feel*: Glad that God always knows everything.

What your students should *do*:
Unsaved: Accept God's plan of salvation.
Saved: Thank God that He is all-knowing.

Lesson outline (for the teacher's and students' notebooks):
1. A better law (Esther 8:1-17).
2. An important victory (Esther 9:1-19).
3. A special celebration (Esther 9:20-32).
4. A new prime minister (Esther 10:1-3).

The verse to be memorized:
God . . . knows all things. (1 John 3:20)

THE LESSON

Haman was dead. Everyone knew that. They had seen him hanging on the gallows he had built.

Haman had decreed that all Jews should die. Instead, Haman was dead. What about his wicked law? Was that dead also?

King Ahasuerus had snatched his ring from Haman. He gave it instead to Mordecai. The king gave everything Haman owned to Queen Esther. And Esther put Mordecai in charge of it.

The Jews should have been happy. Instead, they were crying. Why? Let us peek into the palace.

Two servant girls sat at the door of Queen Esther's room. From behind heavy curtains they could hear her sobbing.

"Why is the queen crying?" one whispered to the other. "Haman is dead. She should be glad. Besides, the king has given all Haman's wealth to her. That should make her happy!"

The other maid whispered, "Haman is dead, that is true. But his law is not dead. Remember? It was sealed with the king's ring. That means the law is still in effect. And a Persian law can never be changed. Never! All Jews in the kingdom will be slain. And that includes our queen, for she, too, is Jewish."

At that moment, the curtains parted and Esther stood before them. "I am going to see the king," she announced. "Will you please help me get ready?" Silently the maids dressed Queen Esther in her beautiful robes. They watched as she moved smoothly, silently to the throne room.

One maid murmured, "The queen must be in big trouble. The king has not called for her. What will we do if he kills her?"

Esther was not worried this time. She was confident that God knows everything. And He is always in control. The Lord had worked before to save His people. Surely He could do so again.

1. A BETTER LAW
Esther 8:1-17

Queen Esther walked right into the throne room. She did! She really, truly did! She fell at the king's feet, crying. "O king!" she begged. "Do not let my people be slaughtered. Please get rid of Haman's wicked law. I cannot bear to have my people destroyed!"

The king held out his golden scepter. But he shook his head sadly. "The laws of the Persians cannot be changed," he said.

Thinking awhile he added, "But there is something I can do. I shall allow Mordecai to make a new law. He can tell the Jews whatever he wishes. He will seal his new law with my ring. Then Mordecai's law can never be broken."

The royal secretaries were called at once. They wrote out Mordecai's law for the Jews. This law said, "All Jews are allowed to defend themselves. They can kill any enemies who try to attack them. They should destroy all the families of their enemies. Jews should take for themselves all that belongs to their enemies. This law will begin on the same day as Haman's law."

Show Illustration #13

Mordecai sealed the law with the king's ring. So this law could not be changed. Never!

Do you remember how Haman had chosen the date for his law? *(By throwing dice.)* The Lord had controlled the dice-rolling: Haman's date was almost a year in the future. Four months had passed. But enough time was left to distribute Mordecai's law. Skilled riders sped on horseback, mules, and camels. They went to all 127 provinces in the kingdom. They spread the good news to every Jewish family. "All Jews can assemble and defend themselves. You can destroy and kill anyone who attacks you. Safeguard yourself, your wife, and your children. Get ready to protect yourselves!" The Jews were delighted. They shouted happily and had great feasts. They could defend themselves!

The Persians and those of other nationalities were terrified. Indeed, some professed to be Jews so they would be safe. (See Esther 8:17.)

After making the law, Mordecai received royal robes. He was given a large golden crown. And all the Jews in Susa, the capital city, celebrated.

2. AN IMPORTANT VICTORY
Esther 9:1-19

For months, the Persians were preparing to slaughter the Jews. They sharpened their weapons. Battle plans were made. At the same time, the Jews were arming themselves against the Persians. The 13th day of the month of Adar came.

Show Illustration #14

In every province the Jews and their enemies clashed. But no one could kill the Jews! At the end of the day thousands of Persians lay dead. The Jews counted those they had destroyed. A thousand in this province. Two thousand there. Five thousand elsewhere in the kingdom. Altogether 75,000 of those who hated the Jews were destroyed. But the Jews did not take anything from their dead enemies.

In Susa, the capital, 500 Persians were slain. But the Jews did not take the belongings of their enemies.

That night the king heard the reports of the Jews' victory. He said to Queen Esther, "Is there anything else you want? I shall give you whatever you ask."

"O king! Will you allow the fighting to continue in Susa another day? And will you have Haman's 10 sons hanged on the gallows?"

The king gladly agreed. So in Susa the battle raged another day. The Jews killed 300 more Persians. But they did not take any of their enemies' belongings. And the 10 sons of Haman, who were already killed, hung on gallows for all to see.

3. A SPECIAL CELEBRATION
Esther 9:20-32

Finally the battle was over. And the Jews enjoyed a great feast. Everyone was happy. Mordecai wrote down all the happenings. He sent letters throughout the empire.

Show Illustration #15

Everywhere the Jews listened to his letter. It read: "Every year, on the fourteenth and fifteenth day of Adar, celebrate. We Jews destroyed our enemies on those dates. Our sorrow was turned to gladness. You should feast and rejoice during the celebration. Send food to one another. Give gifts to the poor." This is exactly what the Jews did. And they remembered Haman and his wicked law.

More than 2,500 years have passed since Esther lived. The Jewish people have suffered many hardships. Others since Haman have tried to destroy them. Indeed, millions of Jews have been massacred. Even so, God's people live throughout all the world. Many thousands have returned to their homeland–Israel.

But wherever Jews are, once every year they celebrate Purim. Haman had determined the date for killing Jews by tossing dice (purim). So Esther called the celebration "Purim." In dramas, they tell Esther's story during Purim. They play games and sing special songs. Children write "Haman" on the soles of their shoes. Then they stamp their feet to erase his name. People eat little triangular pastries called "Haman's hats." It is a very important time on the Jewish calendar. The Jews remember that God saved them from wicked Haman's law. And they enjoy great happiness because of Queen Esther's bravery.

Later, Queen Esther and Mordecai wrote another letter to the Jews. Again they stressed the importance of celebrating Purim. "In addition," they wrote, "do as we do. Spend time fasting. (Do not eat or drink.)" The Jews had fasted when Haman was determined to destroy them. And they prayed. Oh, how they prayed! And they had been saved from destruction. So fasting and prayer were to be observed during Purim.

4. A NEW PRIME MINISTER
Esther 10:1-3

Show Illustration #16

Mordecai had great concern for his people, the Jews. He had fasted and prayed for them during times of crisis. Prayer was a pattern of life for him.

King Ahasuerus honored Mordecai with a promotion. He–a Jew!–became second to the king over the Persian empire. His deeds were written in their history books. (See Esther 10:2.) He was neither proud nor self-centered. He was helpful to his people–God's people–the Jews.

The last verse in the book of Esther says: "Mordecai, the Jew, was next unto King Ahasuerus, and great among the Jews. He was accepted by the multitude of his (Jewish) brethren, seeking the welfare of his people, and speaking peace to all his nation."

The One who knows everything was unknown by the Persians. They honored their king as a god. But Mordecai knew and prayed to the true and living God. And the God of Heaven heard and answered Mordecai's prayers.

A good man and wise was Mordecai. Esther had been entrusted to his care when her parents died. And Mordecai took this responsibility seriously. He knew she was surrounded by heathen people in the palace. She could not speak of God there. Nor would she have been queen had her nationality been known! So Mordecai had commanded her not to mention that she was Jewish. God knew Mordecai would guide Esther wisely.

Esther respected Mordecai, her foster father. She, the queen, always obeyed him. She fasted and prayed–right there in the palace. She called upon all Jews to pray for their protection. And they obeyed her. From the beginning God knew Esther would honor Him. He knew He could use Esther to protect the Jews. Indeed, many thousands were spared from death because of young Esther.

Why did God choose the Jews for Himself? He loved them. Though most Jews have turned from Him, He still loves them. God chose to send His Son to earth through a Jewish family. God's Son, the Lord Jesus Christ, lived an absolutely perfect life. He always did that which pleased His Father in Heaven. He never, never, never did one wrong thing. He never had a wrong thought. Not one!

God sent His "Son to be the Saviour of the world." (See 1 John 4:14.) To save people, the Son of God had to die. He had to take all the punishment for all our sins. The Son of God, the Lord Jesus Christ, did die. He "bore our sins in His own body" when He died. (See 1 Peter 2:24.) "All we like sheep have gone astray; we have turned every one to his own way. And the Lord [God] has laid on Him [the Lord Jesus Christ] the iniquity [sin] of us all" (Isaiah 53:6).

"God so loved the world, that He gave His only begotten Son, that whosoever believeth in Him should not perish, but have everlasting life" (John 3:16).

Do you believe that the Lord Jesus Christ is the Son of God? Do you believe He died for *you*? Will you receive Him as your Saviour? Will you do so right now?

When you receive the Lord Jesus, God receives you. (See John 1:12.) You become a child of God, a member of His family. He, the true and living God of Heaven, will be your Father. He is a loving, wise Father who cares for His own. He, the omniscient (all-knowing) One, will care for *you*.